# Daddy's Wicked Parties

The Most Shocking True Story of
Child Abuse Ever Told

## Disclaimer

This book is based on true events.

The names of people and places have been changed to protect the innocent.

Cover photograph is posed by a model and is used for illustrative purposes only

# CONTENTS

# *A Note from Kate*

It may seem a funny thing for a child abuse victim to want to relive past horrors, to recall the intimate details of the worst parts of her life. But I do understand it. For I, too, am a victim of abuse.

I have scoured the bookstores and bestseller lists for stories of child abuse. I have tuned in to the late-night documentaries on the most horrific abuse cases. I know that, far from avoiding all mention of abuse, we victims often seek it out, looking, searching for something: justice, vindication, empathy, connection. Sometimes in reading the stories of others I have felt the greatest comfort of all.

I know that telling one's own story, getting it all down on paper gives a type of vindication, a catharsis that allows a lot of the horror to be let go. Perhaps one day, I will find the courage to publish my own disturbing memoir.

Lucy and I had been friends and confidants for some years before we made the decision to write a book together detailing the shocking story of her early life. Although this is the second book published in the Skylark True Child Abuse series, it was actually written some time before the first book, *Dirty Little Dog.*

When I interviewed Lucy for this book, she spoke only in the present tense, as if the events were happening now. She spoke as an adult, but sometimes with the words of a child. As if it were still so fresh in her mind that the memory was still completely present. I decided to preserve that sense of immediacy and have kept her words in the present tense.

I have changed very little of Lucy's story. Obviously, names and places are changed to protect the innocent, and I have edited and altered sections for the sake of understanding and readability. But for the main part, these words are Lucy's, just as she told them to me.

# Lucy's Story

*When you see a child walking, perhaps looking happy, perhaps looking forlorn – a beautiful innocent little child – you can never know what lurks in its once pure and sweet mind; you know not what monsters haunt its thoughts and dreams. Child sexual abuse is so prevalent that, statistically speaking, every one of us has looked into the face of a secretly abused child. Just think about that as you look around the streets of your hometown. Some of those children you see have been abused, are being abused, or will be abused tonight for the very first time. That thought makes me so sick I can hardly bear it.*

*Perhaps one day you saw a particular little girl walking home from school on a Friday afternoon in*

*North London. She would have appeared like any normal little ten-year-old girl. A bit taller than average. Brown straight hair. Rumpled blue dress. Crooked front teeth.*

*She would have been dawdling along, dragging her tired feet, her bag slung over one shoulder. If you happened to notice her, you probably imagined her weariness was just down to ordinary tiredness after a long day. Perhaps inside she is filled with excitement and relief that the weekend is upon her with all its promise of fun and entertainment.*

*But not this little girl. She is in no hurry to get home. She is doing her best to make the journey last as long as she can. As she turns the corner into her own street, she starts to feel a familiar dread: it is Friday once again and the weekend is here. There will be no picnics for her this weekend; no friends to stay, no trips to the zoo or the beach, no visiting granny or watching films at the pictures.*

*But there will be a party. Oh, yes, there will be a party...*

# Chapter 1

I am about ten when it starts. Mum is still living with us at this point. We live in a tiny terraced house in a suburb of North London. The house is scruffy and has tattered wallpaper. We only have a little television set and no telephone. The carpet on the lounge floor is stained and has bare patches. In some places the floorboards show through. We don't have a proper garden – just a back yard full of old ladders and tins of paint.

But this first little house is 'the happy house'. The few good memories I have from childhood are all from my time here. I don't mind one bit that the house is small and tatty. I don't care that my bedroom is so tiny it is hardly bigger than a cupboard. Children never care about those sorts of things. It's my home, simple as that.

My dad works at a factory. He drives a forklift truck, which is a very dangerous job. But Dad doesn't belong at the factory. He always tells me he could have been a scientist or a doctor or something. He could have gone to university and got a degree if he had had the chance. But university is only for rich, stuck-up posh people and not for working-class men like him, he tells me.

Dad is a bit fat, and when he wears a t-shirt his hairy belly hangs over the top of his trousers. His trousers always fall down at the back and when he bends over you can see the top of his bum crack. He's very hairy and even has black hair on the tops of his shoulders and on his back. His hair is black and he has it cut really short all over. He looks quite scary when he has first had it cut but it's nice to touch. Sometimes I like to sit on his lap and run my hand across the back of his head, stroking his hair like cat fur.

My mum is a nurse at the casualty department of the hospital in town. She is very kind and clever too. But Dad always tells me she is not as clever as him even though she has a master's degree. I remember her laughing a lot when I was small but these days she seems to be sad most of the time. She gets into a lot of arguments with Dad and he often loses his temper with her. When she gets upset she picks bits of skin off her lips and licks them over and over. They go really red and sometimes a line of blood appears when she has picked too much.

Mum is very, very skinny. She likes to wear long skirts and flat shoes. She only has tiny boobs, and when she bends over she looks like a blade of grass or a straw bending in the middle. Everything about Mum is long. She has a long nose and long, straggly blonde hair. Sometimes I think she looks a bit like a witch, but a nice witch.

I don't have any brothers or sisters and I don't really mind that. One time Mum told me she was having a baby and that I was going to have a brother or sister. But she never ended up having the baby. When I asked her about it she told me that some little babies aren't meant to be born, and that this one had gone now. There were a lot of arguments when I thought Mum was having a baby.

Mum often has to work funny hours, doing shift work – sometimes she works all day or all night. I am often left alone to look after myself, and

I have to let myself into the house through the back door after school. I don't need my own key because nobody locks their back door. I never have a babysitter or child-minder but I can go to Mrs Watts's house next door if I need anything. Sometimes I go and watch TV in her house until Mum or Dad get home. But mostly I prefer to be on my own. I'm not bothered by it; I'm so used to being alone after school and to be honest, I quite like it.

I can't run in the back garden because it's too small but I can skip out there and play 'elastic'. At school we play in groups of three, with two girls holding the elastic around their legs while the third girl has her turn jumping over it. When I'm playing on my own I pass the big loop of elastic around the backs of two kitchen chairs. I say a rhyme as I jump: *England, Ireland, Scotland, Wales, Inside, Outside, Inside, ON!* You have to land with your feet on the two strips of elastic as you say the last word.

One Friday after school I return home to find the house empty, as usual. I come through the unlocked back door into the kitchen, sling my school bag over the back of one of the kitchen chairs and go straight to the fridge. I am always ravenous after school and I want a snack. Finding jam and butter in the fridge and bread in the bread bin, I make myself a jam sandwich, standing up on the little step that lets me reach the kitchen worktop. I take a bag of crisps from the cupboard, and with my snack and a glass of squash I go into the lounge to watch television until my mother comes home.

I watch TV for a few hours. Mum is not due home until much later and Dad is nowhere to be seen. I get a bit bored with TV so I start wandering about the house, looking in cupboards and poking around in the spare bedroom. This room is full of storage boxes and I always enjoy snooping through them, discovering old toys and interesting forgotten objects. Once I even found a nest of baby mice in there. I wanted to keep them as pets but Dad said they were dirty and put them out in the back yard to live. Sometimes I put little bits of cheese out for them and sit very still on the back step to see if the mice will come out. But I never see them.

The one room that is totally out of bounds to me is my parents' bedroom. I am forbidden to enter this room without their permission. Of course, this makes it all the more mysterious and exciting. It's almost as if the room calls to me to creep in and look about. And their order to stay away hasn't prevented me from occasionally stepping inside and opening the odd wardrobe door before being overcome with a feeling of wrongdoing, hurriedly leaving and quietly closing the door. This particular evening I have no intention of doing anything but exactly this. But that's not the way it turns out.

I turn the handle on my parents' door and push it. The room opens before me, neat and tidy, as always. My mum knows how to keep my dad happy. If the house is a mess he gets very upset and shouts at her. So she always keeps the house nice. She's kind like that.

I look around the room. The bed is made. The curtains are pulled back. There are no clothes or papers on the floor, no empty cups on the dresser or books left out. The room is immaculate, all except one thing. There is one drawer in my mother's bedside table that's open, open quite wide. This one open drawer looks strangely out of place amongst the tidiness of the room. It seems to beckon to me, drawing me to walk up and investigate what it is trying to reveal to me.

I step warily inside the room, feeling tingly and self-conscious in my crime, tiptoeing across the carpet as if Mum and Dad could somehow hear my footsteps from wherever they are. I go straight up to the open drawer and peer in. There's a woman's magazine at the top that almost fills the entire area of the drawer, *Family Circle*. Mum reads this magazine all the time. It usually has a picture of a cake on the front. The magazine is not sitting flat. It's doing a very poor job of concealing what is clearly a whole drawerful of contents underneath it.

I take out the *Family Circle,* lay it on the bed and start to inspect the objects my mother has tried very absentmindedly to hide. There are several bottles of pills with my mum's name on them, *Mrs. J Gilbert,* and a jar or two of face cream, some bits and pieces of jewellery and a hairbrush. There is a blue and white tube of some sort of lotion with the letters KY on it. There's also a long, thin plastic cylinder, creamy white and tapered at one end. It's heavy, like it must have electrical workings or batteries inside. I take it out and put it on the bed. I can see that the rest of the drawer is filled simply with more magazines.

I am about to put everything back and turn away when I catch a better look at the front of the topmost magazine. I'm shocked to see that it has a half-naked lady on its cover. She has her eyes closed and her face is scrunched up like she is trying really hard to lift something heavy. I take out the magazine, seeing that there are half a dozen or more similar ones underneath.

At that moment, I hear a noise. The creak of the front gate as someone opens it. My mother is home! In a rush, I throw the tube of KY and the white cylinder back into the drawer. I put the *Family Circle* back on top, just as it had been when I found it. But then I realise: the naked lady magazine is still out! I try to shove it back under the *Family Circle* and the other objects but I am panicking and clumsy. As I hear the back door open I have no choice but to close the drawer as it was, snatch up the magazine, run from the room and close the door. As I do, I hear my mother coming through the kitchen and start up the stairs. I just have time to get into my own room, close the door, throw the magazine down the side of my bed against the wall and lie on the bed before my mother reaches the landing.

'Oh, here you are,' she says, opening the door. 'What are you doing up here in the dark?'

'You're so late,' I ignore her question. 'I didn't know when you were coming back.'

We both go downstairs to watch television until Dad comes home. I forget all about the mystery magazine down the side of my bed.

*When I think back, it always feels that this is the day when it all started to go wrong for me.*

*Until this point I remember mainly the good things, the laughing, the love, the birthday presents. I remember riding around on my father's back as he crawls around the floor like a horse, my mother watching and laughing. Playing in the snow with the two of them holding my hands on either side. All three of us falling flat on our backs in a snowdrift, completely unhurt. My granny bringing me a bowl of Sugar Puffs in my bedroom while I am very sick with mumps. She reads to me while Mum does funny actions for the characters in the book. These are the happy times of my childhood. I cling to these memories like treasures. They keep me safe at night when I feel the bad thoughts looming.*

*But after this day the memories seem to have all turned sour. For a long time I believed that I had been the cause of all the trouble, that everything that went on to happen had been my fault. After all, if I hadn't snooped around on that day I would not have set in motion that series of terrible events.*

*I know now that none of this was my fault. But even today, when I look back, it seems like the clouds drew over the sky on that day and didn't part again for many years.*

# Chapter 2

It is not until the following day at school that I
remember the magazine. I am very nervous all day.
I know I'm going to be in real trouble if my parents
ever find it because they will know I have been
snooping around in their forbidden room. There's a
real danger of my mother finding it while she's
cleaning, and my mother cleans a lot. I resolve to
put it back as soon as I get home that night.

When I get home after school I go straight up
to my room and retrieve the magazine from its
hiding place. Its pages have become scrunched and
folded back when I threw it down by the side of
my bed in my rush to hide it. I try to smooth them
back as best I can.

Then, just out of curiosity, I turn the first page. Then I turn another, and another.

I have a little knowledge about sex, picked up from television and other children. I know where babies come from and I have seen animals mating on nature programmes. But in the pages of that magazine I see the most bewildering images. I see women with men's penises in their mouths. I see people having sex in all sorts of positions. It's shocking and makes me feel a little bit sick. But the images are also fascinating. I am appalled and sickened but engrossed at the same time by the sheer badness of what I'm seeing. I know I will be in terrible, terrible trouble if ever my mum and dad find out that I have taken this magazine. And, somehow, that just makes me want to look even more.

It is fully my intention to return the magazine to its proper place and forget all about it. I never intended to go back into my mother's room, open the drawer, see the other pornographic magazines and swap the one I had for the next one in the pile.

But that is exactly what I do. And another evening is spent in sick, horrified fascination, poring over a second obscene magazine. I do the same the next night.

After a week or so of this, I have become much braver and I no longer feel like such a criminal. The lack of fear means I stop being so careful when in my parents' forbidden room, sometimes taking two magazines.

Then the fateful day comes: I become so complacent and unafraid that I take the whole stack. What a silly thing to do! It will now be completely obvious that they are all missing rather than just one or two. But these thoughts don't even cross my mind. And, of course, it is that very night that Mum discovers my crime.

It's late and I'm in bed already when I hear her go to her room. I hear her walking about undressing, putting things away. The floor creaks, things rustle, cupboard doors open and close. Then I hear a gasp and an 'Oh no!' Then she shrieks, 'Steve! Come here, now!'

My father comes up the stairs and goes into the bedroom. I hear hushed voices, and then the door slams shut. More hushed voices, murmuring through the wall. My mother is crying now. And my father is talking angrily. I can hear his raised voice.

I know what has happened. My mother has noticed the magazines are gone. My crime has been discovered and I'm in deep, terrible trouble. I pull the bedclothes over my head so that I can't hear the voices any more. I lie there, expecting that at any moment my door will burst open and I will have to face the music. I curl up tight in a ball, facing away from the door, facing the side of the bed and its guilty secret. I wish I had never snooped; I wish I had never even opened that bedroom door in the first place. I wish I had just stayed watching television that night.

But my parents do not come into my room that night, and I soon fall asleep. Not a word is said about the matter as I get up and go to school. Perhaps they haven't discovered my secret after all. Perhaps the argument and shouting last night are about something completely different. Perhaps I can even return the magazines and no one will ever know my crime.

On returning home from school, I go to my bedroom to find that all the magazines are gone from the side of my bed. I don't go anywhere near my parents' room that evening but just sit and anxiously watch television until they return.

Mum and Dad have both come home earlier than usual. They have brought back fish and chips for dinner. They aren't angry at all. Instead it almost seems like they're being extra kind to me. Perhaps I didn't do anything wrong after all. Perhaps I am going to get away with it. Perhaps they were arguing about something else last night.

After dinner, Mum clears everything away and Dad turns off the television.

'Janice, go in the other room,' he says to Mum. 'I want to talk to Lucy.'

'Steve, please don't…' she begins, but he cuts her off.

'Will you keep out of this and do as you are fucking told?' His voice has its really angry sound. I know she will do as she is told when he speaks like that. When he swears she goes quiet. Sometimes when he speaks like that he gets so angry that he pushes her against the wall.

'And close the door!' he orders as she leaves the room.

Then Dad smiles at me and says, 'Come here, Lucy. Come and sit with Daddy.' I leave the floor where I'm sitting and join him on the sofa.

'Lucy, you've been in Mummy and Daddy's room, haven't you?' My heart leaps and I nod, afraid.

'I wasn't being bad. I was just looking,' I tell him.

'I know that, Lucy. I know you aren't a bad girl.' I relax a little. 'I know you were looking at Mummy's magazines. But that's fine. Did you like those magazines? Did you like the pictures in them?'

I shake my head.

'Did you just think they were interesting? Is that why you took them all to look at?'

I nod. He tells me he's glad. He tells me I'm a big, grown-up girl and that lots of girls wouldn't be interested because they're just silly little babies. I feel instantly brighter. My dad is such a wonderful dad. He does sometimes shout at Mum but is always so kind to me. He understands me. He understands that I was just interested in the magazines and that I wasn't really being bad.

Then he tells me to look at the magazines whenever I want. And if I like, I can look at the ones in *his* drawer too. Those ones are different, he says, and he thinks I'll like them.

My dad really is amazing. He can always take a bad situation and make it better.

It's Friday night and the school week is over. I thought I was in such trouble but Mum and Dad give me the most wonderful weekend possible. They take me shopping to buy new clothes and then take me out to visit Berkhamsted Castle. Dad always drives. He doesn't approve of Mum driving and he shouts at other women drivers all the time. At Berkhamsted there's a woman trying to park in a tiny space in the car park. She has a really big, posh car, and she's taking a long time to get into the space. Dad is so angry.

'Don't go borrowing your husband's car if you don't know how to drive it!' he shouts at her. The lady looks shocked that Dad was shouting at her but I don't think she heard what he said. Sometimes I get a bit embarrassed of Dad in public.

But we have such a good time at the castle. Dad runs around the ruins pretending to be a knight and I'm a princess being attacked by a dragon. He shouts, 'I'll save you!' as he slays the dragon with a big sweep of his pretend sword. 'The beast is dead! Your kingdom is safe, Princess Lucy!' He bows in front of me. I love him so much. I sometimes wish I could marry him when I'm older, but I know you can't marry your own family.

In the evening they take me out to a really posh restaurant in one of my new dresses. The waiter calls me 'Madam' and pulls my chair out before I sit down. When I do sit down, he lays a thick, white cotton napkin across my lap. I eat Chicken Maryland, which Dad said is Kentucky Fried Chicken for posh people. I feel like the luckiest girl in the world.

They don't say anything more about the magazines all weekend. But on Sunday night I'm in bed when I hear them arguing in their room again. Mum is crying. I sit up in my bed with my knees up, wishing I could hear one of them say something nice to the other. I pull a long strand of hair around to the front of my face and chew on it. I do this a lot.

'You can't make her look at those, she's too young!' she says in a wobbly voice.

Dad is shouting at Mum. He's telling her he's not making me do anything, that it's up to me if I want to look at the magazines. She just keeps saying, 'She's too young! She's just a child.' Dad keeps on shouting until I hear a clumping noise, like Mum has fallen over.

'Mum, are you okay?' I shout. Dad comes instantly to my room to reassure me. 'Mummy's fine, darling. She just slipped a bit. You go back to sleep.' I am a bit worried that Mum has hurt herself. But at least she has Dad to look after her.

*I thought they were so happy and in love. I thought my mum and dad were the most perfect couple ever. Why would I have thought anything different? All mums and dads loved each other, didn't they? And I loved them both so much.*

# Chapter 3

Mum has swapped her shifts so that she's home every day after school. I discover that it's actually nice to have Mum smiling at me when I come in through the back door, rather than being left alone. She knows I'm always hungry after school, and sometimes she even has a sandwich already made for me when I come in. I start to love having her there to look after me in the evenings, rather than being left to look after myself all the time. She may not be as clever as Dad, but I still love her so much. And she does seem to be learning to be a better mum. She does whatever Dad tells her, so I know she is trying hard.

Tonight is the first night that Mum has to go back to her old shift again. I'm going to be alone after school for the first time in a while. Mum tells me in the morning and sends me off to school with a big hug.

'And, Lucy, remember you don't have to look at those magazines if you don't want to,' she says. I look surprised at her. It's really funny because I had forgotten all about them.

'You don't have to do *anything* if you don't want to. Okay?' she says to me in such a serious voice it almost makes me laugh.

Silly Mummy. I don't know why she's so bothered about this. Perhaps she thinks I'm just a little girl who can't make up her own mind about things. But I'm not a baby. I'm ten years old and I'm very, very mature. Dad always tells me that. I resolve to look at Dad's magazines tonight, just to show her and Dad how grown up and mature I really am.

That evening after school I go up to Mum and Dad's room. I enter the room without any hesitation whatsoever and go straight to his side of the bed. I open his drawer and find it stuffed full of magazines too. He doesn't even have all the other bits and pieces like Mum does. I take a few of the magazines out. Dad's magazines are quite different from the ones Mum has. These look more like just scrapbooks with photographs stuck in them. I can also see a lot of single photos just loose in the drawer. Some are black-and-white. The photographs are not as clear and bright as those in Mum's magazines and some of them are quite blurry. Some are dark or much too light, and the people have red eyes; they're more like the ordinary photos in our family album. The men in Dad's photos are doing the same sorts of things as in Mum's magazines. But I can see one very big difference between Dad's scrapbook and Mum's magazines.

All of Dad's photos also have children in them.

There are a few little boys, but almost all of the children are girls. Most of them look just a bit older than me, maybe about eleven or twelve. One little girl is bending over to show her naked bottom, and she only looks about five years old.

I put all the photos and the scrapbooks back in the drawer and leave the room. I don't want to take them back to my room and look at them again. I kind of wish I hadn't seen them at all. I feel a bit funny and a bit shocked. Why does Dad want to look at these? Why does he want *me* to look at them? Aren't these children all being very naughty and so *rude*? Aren't the grown-ups doing something bad too? Everyone always says that sex is something only mums and dads do to each other. It isn't *for* children. We aren't even allowed to talk about it because it's too rude. I have been told that a million times. I'm not sure what I'm supposed to think or what to do. And I don't know what I'm going to say to Mum when she comes home.

I hear her open the back door and come down to face her. But it's not Mum standing there to greet me. For the first time ever, Dad has come home before Mum. I'm surprised but quite happy to see him. I know that now Dad is home he will make it all better; Dad always makes it better.

He smiles at me, and just says, 'Did you look in my drawer?' I nod shyly, looking away from him. I feel a bit embarrassed and I don't know what to say.

'Excellent! I knew you would. You're such a good girl. Now, I want to have a talk with you before Mummy gets home. Go up to our bedroom and wait for me.'

I do as I'm told and go into Mum and Dad's room and sit on the bed. Dad comes up a few minutes later with a tray of hot chocolate, crisps and marshmallow teacakes. He knows they're my favourite!

While we're eating, Dad opens the drawer and takes out one of the scrapbooks. He sits down beside me and opens the book on his knees so we can both see clearly. He turns the pages until he gets to a page with three photos of little girls with no clothes on. None of them is doing sex things; they are just naked. Two of them are sitting on the floor, facing the camera with their legs apart. I feel hot and uncomfortable looking at these pictures in front of my dad. But he doesn't seem at all embarrassed.

'Aren't they pretty?' says Dad. 'Aren't they beautiful children, Lucy?'

It's true. These little girls look like angels. But they are still being quite naughty sitting there showing themselves to the camera like that.

'But, Dad,' I protest. 'They're naked. Aren't they being rude?'

Dad shakes his head. He says that's just what silly stupid people think. Then he tells me that these children are professionals. They're making a lot of money as actors and models. They pose for these photos because they want to and they get paid for it. They are like actors on the telly, he says: like superstars. Dad says something can't be okay for adults, but rude and bad for children. He says that's not rational. Dad always has a different way of looking at things.

He tells me that politicians have made laws to stop children from working even though sometimes their parents don't even have enough food to eat or have any clothes to wear, and the good little children want to help. Everyone knows politicians are bad and make up stupid laws that make people's lives a misery. I hear people say things like this all the time. Those politicians should listen to people like my dad. Sometimes Dad says *he* should have been a politician.

'So do you like these photos, Lucy?' he asks.

'I don't know,' I shrug. 'They're alright.' I really don't like them at all; they make me feel weird, but I so want to please my dad.

'I've got lots more of these photos for you to see. I have some films too. You'll love those.' As he puts the photos away he says, 'I'm going to come home from work early from now on. So we can watch films together.'

Now Dad comes home early every night, just after I get back from school. Every night he makes me a delicious tea with cakes and crisps, and he shows me photos upstairs or films downstairs on the video. He talks to me too, telling me all about what the children's names are and how long they have been working. He has some favourite actresses and some that he doesn't like so much. But they are all superstars, he tells me. Lots of them look foreign. I ask Dad if they're Chinese but he says they're from the Philippines. In places like the Philippines and Thailand, he tells me, it's normal for children to have sex and no one thinks there's anything wrong with it. It's completely allowed there, he says. How could something be wrong in one country and not in another, he asks me. I don't reply.

One day, Dad says, the world will understand and it will change. When that happens, Dad tells me, children will be allowed to do sex whenever they want and with anyone they want, and the child stars will be recognised for the wonderful work they do.

Usually, when we have watched films or looked at photos, Dad tells me it's bath time. My dad has always bathed me, for as long as I can remember. But I didn't used to have a bath every night like I do now.

He always washes me all over very slowly, cleaning me very carefully and thoroughly with lots of soap to make sure I am properly clean. He spends a long time doing this, paying a lot of attention to washing between my legs. You can get awful diseases if you don't wash your money box properly, diseases that can kill you or make it so that you can't have babies when you grow up. That's what Dad tells me.

*Mum tells me he had a way of making out that she was the weird one. That she was the sick, wrong one. He would tell her that it was our repressed society that refused to acknowledge children's sexuality. He would claim that those who denied children's sexuality were the real monsters, the real perverts.*

*He always used to tell her that looking wasn't a crime. After all, he told her, there was no helping these children in the pictures, and not to look would be like refusing to eat an animal that has already been killed.*

*Did you really believe that crap, Dad? Did you really think it was true that it was the whole world that was wrong, not you and your friends?*

*I really doubt that.*

# Chapter 4

One night, we have just watched one of 'those' films and it is quite late in the evening. Dad runs the bath as usual and puts me in it. But this time, Dad does something different. He takes all his clothes off and gets into the bath with me. It's so funny having Dad in the bath with me with his big, hairy belly showing. It makes me laugh. After he has cleaned me he shows me how he washes his own penis with lots and lots of soap to make sure it is really clean. After that first time, Dad gets in the bath with me every time. Sometimes he makes me wash him back, just so I know how to do it properly. He says it's good practise. I don't really like washing Dad's bits even though he says it's okay. It doesn't feel right. And I just know Mum won't like it if she finds out. But he only does it when she's out of the house. Dad says Mum wouldn't understand and she'd only get upset if she knew. So it's best not to tell her.

We've been having a bath together almost every evening for a long time now. Tonight we're almost finished and about to get out when I hear the back door open. Mum is home early.

'What are you doing back?' Dad shouts down the stairs to her.

'Had an accident with a drunk patient,' she says, coming up the stairs. 'Cut myself. It's really deep. Had to get two stitches. They sent me home.'

She's upstairs in no time. I look at Dad in horror but he doesn't move. I hear her pause outside the bathroom before opening the door. Dad is sitting naked in the bath with me. She stands at the doorway of the bathroom and her mouth falls wide open and she breathes in deeply. Her cut hand goes up to cover it. The hand is covered in a white bandage.

'What have you done to her?' she screams. 'Have you…?'

'I haven't bloody touched her, you mad cow!' he bawls back at her, getting up soaking from the bath. His penis is sticking straight up in the air.

'You're sick!' she tells him. 'She's just a little girl!'

'You're the one that's sick!' shouts Dad. 'I'll show you how sick I am, shall I?' I hear her shouting 'No!' and I see him dragging her towards the bedroom. I get out of the bath and wrap myself in my favourite pink towel. I follow Mum and Dad to the bedroom but to my shock, Dad slams the door in my face. I hear muffled shouting and squealing from Mum and the sound of the bed creaking. I think they're having sex with each other

I feel a bit better now that I can hear that. I know that sex is what people do when they love each other, so they can't be arguing any more. I dry myself and put some pyjamas on while the thumps and bed-creaking continue, and then I go downstairs to watch television.

When Mum comes down the stairs, she has a big red bruise on her cheek. I hadn't realised she hit her face at work as well as her hand. The injured hand is bleeding badly, right through the bandage.

After that day when Mum found us in the bath, Dad always washes me every night even when she is in the house. He says now that she knows he has nothing to hide. He always puts me to bed too, rubbing lotion onto me while I lay there, to keep my skin soft.

I wish Mum would try harder to stop annoying Dad. He has such a temper and sometimes he says he has to hit her because she winds him up so much. I hate that. I know Dad is very clever but I don't think he should hit Mum like he does. He could just shout at her and she will still do as she is told. He doesn't need to hit her too. I wish he wouldn't. She cries all the time. One day when I ask him to stop hitting Mum, he just shouts at her even more. He says, 'You see what you're doing to her, you crazy bitch! Can't you keep your shit away from our daughter?'

Dad tells Mum she needs professional help and that he's taking her to get 'sorted out'. I am really afraid that Dad is going to call the police and get her in trouble, but it turns out he's just taking her to see a doctor. The doctor gives her some pills. They make her really quiet and sleepy, but she must be feeling better because she has stopped crying. She doesn't argue with Dad when she takes the pills, and Dad isn't hitting her any more. That makes me really happy.

# DADDY'S WICKED PARTIES

Mum and Dad have gone on holiday for a week. They say they're going to 'patch things up' and they've left me with my granny to look after me. She comes down and stays with me whenever Mum and Dad go away. Dad makes me promise not to say a single word to her about the magazines or the films or the baths. He says she'll only cause a lot of trouble if she knows.

Granny lives in Scotland, where Mum was born. She has a strong Scottish accent and she calls me 'hen' or 'henny'. She says it means 'darling'. I like it when she calls me that. I always think of a big, really fluffy chicken when she says it. I almost tell her about the magazines because I think she would understand. She is so lovely. But I don't because Dad made me promise.

I love it when Granny comes to stay. She has a little white Westie dog called Pickles and I love playing with him and taking him out for walks on my own.

But Granny always cooks weird food and makes me eat strange cereal for breakfast. She gives me courgettes for the first time and I think they're fried cucumbers. She also makes a pot of tea to drink with dinner instead of water or squash. But she also makes loads of lovely cakes and sweets. I always beg her to make 'tablet'. That's not medicine – it's a bit like fudge. You can't get it in England.

Dad doesn't like Granny very much. He says she's a meddler. But Granny isn't scared of Dad like Mum is. She says if he tries anything while she's around she'll knock him down and he won't get up again. She's not like a proper old lady granny; she wears jeans.

But when Mum and Dad get back from holiday and Granny goes home, they don't seem very happy. Mum is really, really dozy from the medicine she has to take now.

Dad always brings Mum her pills in the evening. He gives her a big drink of gin and tonic, too, and tells her to take her pills with it. She sits there drinking her gin, and then always falls asleep in the armchair in front of the telly. Dad waits for her to fall asleep before he puts me to bed. He sits in my bed with me on his lap, and rubs the lotion onto me while we look at the scrapbooks and photos. He has got lots of new ones now and always has new children to show me and talk to me about. All Dad ever wants to do now is look at these photos of children with me.

Dad says this is the biggest and best secret that I could ever swear to keep. It is only clever people like me and Dad and the children in the photos that understand. It is our secret, a secret only really clever people know about. He says other people just don't understand. They are backward and old-fashioned and repressed, he says. They might even put him in prison, just for letting me look at some photos! How can looking be a crime, says Dad. If my dad went to prison it would be the worst thing in the world. I couldn't bear it if I could never see my dad again. I decide never ever to tell anyone about our secret. I don't tell anyone about the photos. I know they wouldn't understand.

But Dad doesn't know that I really don't like looking at the photos at all. I sometimes think the children look really sad. Some of the men in the photos look ugly and old and dirty. But I don't want to disappoint Dad. I love him spending so much time with me. I just wish we could do something else for a change. I wish we could go out to see a castle like we used to, or to see a film at the pictures. Or just watch television or go to the park or play games.

The photos are starting to make me feel upset, and sometimes, when he is looking at them, Dad is too rough when he rubs the cream in. But Mum isn't crying any more and Dad isn't hitting her. He cuddles me and strokes me and calls me his darling girl. I don't like the photos or the films but things are still okay at the moment. I wish Mum was a bit happier, though.

*I know Mum should have done more. She could have stopped things from escalating. She could still have saved me at this point. So many people over the years have told me this. So many people have expected me to be angry and resentful toward her for not protecting me and stopping him in time. I've heard it so many times.*

*I don't blame my mum at all. I truly believe she felt as trapped as I did.*

*I was there. I know what he was like.*

# Chapter 5

Everything changes in the space of one night. Mum and Dad are at work and I am alone. Then Dad comes home from work later than usual. He has been drinking beer and I can smell the alcohol on his breath. He's different than usual. He doesn't make me any food or call me his darling girl. He just tells me to go to my room. 'It's time, Lucy,' he mumbles. 'You're ready.'

He doesn't say another word. He just tells me to take my clothes off and lie on the bed. I think he is going to rub the cream in but instead he takes off his own trousers and pants and gets into bed with me. I can't believe what is happening. My own Dad gets on top of me in my own little bed and has sex with me for the first time. I hate it. He is really heavy and hot. I cry out and ask him to stop but he is drunk and is paying no attention to me. I try to push against his big, sweaty, hairy chest but he hardly seems to notice. He just carries on. He smells of strong beer and cigarettes, not just his breath but all over his body. I hate that he's drunk, and it scares me how different he is. It's like he isn't really my dad any more; he's almost like a stranger. When it's over he doesn't comfort me or wipe away my tears. He just gets up and off me without saying a word and leaves the room.

I am shaking with the shock and horror of what has just happened. I just lie there crying for ages. Eventually I get up and walk into the hall to see where Dad has gone. His bedroom door is open and I can see that he has fallen asleep, still half dressed, face down on the bed.

I don't know what to do. Dad's like a different person when he's drunk, like some sort of animal or devil. I'm too scared to wake him up. I go back to my room and sit on the bed and cry some more. But then I hear Dad stir and call something out in his drunken sleep.

'Youuuu….fffff…can't…fuckin…'     He's speaking nonsense, but angry nonsense. I'm terrified it is all about to start again, and I frantically throw some clothes on before he has a chance to wake up. I run out of the house and look up and down the street, sobbing hysterically. I have no idea where to go. I think about walking to the hospital where Mum works but I don't know the way. The only person I know well on the street is the next-door neighbour, Mrs Watts. I run around the back of her house and bang on the kitchen door. She opens it quickly and lets me in. Mrs Watts is very nosy and keeps asking me what has happened and what's wrong. But I tell her nothing. I just keep saying that my dad is asleep and that I want my mum. Mrs Watts has a phone. I know Mum's number at work in case of emergencies and Mrs Watts calls her for me. When Mum comes to the phone Mrs Watts passes it to me. I can't say a word but just sob uncontrollably into the receiver.

Mum arrives home in a few minutes. I don't know how she got home so fast. She must have paid for a taxi or sprinted all the way from the hospital. She doesn't say anything much to Mrs Watts. She just says 'thanks' and takes me straight home, ignoring the lady's questions about what's wrong. She takes me into the lounge, shuts the door and sits me down before she says anything at all.

'Lucy, what did he do?' she whispers. She is shaking and her lip is trembling.

'He…he got into bed with me… and he…' I stop and look at her. I can trust Mum because she has seen the photos too. She knows. I can tell her everything. So I tell her what Dad did. I tell her he's drunk and like a monster and how scared I was. She holds my body tight against her and cries and cries into my shoulder. She rocks me back and forth on her lap, crying, 'I'm so sorry, I'm so sorry! I should have stopped him! It will never happen again, Lucy. I'll see to that.'

She sleeps with me in my bed that night. I feel safe with her, and I think perhaps she is not as silly and stupid as Dad says.

The next morning Mum gets me up very early and dresses me quietly. We leave the house before Dad gets up and we get on a bus into town. I think Mum is taking me to do some shopping but instead she takes me to the police station. She talks to the lady at the front desk while I sit across the room on a plastic chair. The police lady opens her eyes very wide and looks shocked. She's very kind and gives Mum a tissue while she makes a phone call. Then she takes us to another room to wait and brings us some tea. Mum comes to sit with me while there's a bit of a commotion going on. Two policemen come into the room to talk to Mum and then go away again. There is a lot of whispering. People keep looking at me and giving me pretend smiles.

'Mum, what's going on?' I ask her. 'Why are we in the police station?'

'I have told the police what Daddy did. It's okay, Lucy. They're going to arrest him and he will never be able to hurt you again.'

I stare at her. Arrest him? I knew what that meant. That meant he was going to prison. What was she thinking of? I thought she understood. How could she do this to Dad?

'But he'll go to prison!' I say horrified.

'Yes, for a long time, with a bit of luck,' she actually smiles. 'And then he'll never be able to hurt us again.'

'How could you do that to Dad?' I shout at her. 'How could you take my Daddy away?' I'm crying again now. 'I hate you! You are mad, just like Daddy said.' I run away from her and sit in the corner of the room.

'I'm sorry, Lucy. It's all for the best. It's all going to be okay now.' She is crying and smiling at the same time.

Eventually, a policewoman comes in to talk to me. She has a pad of paper and a clipboard and lots of pens in the top pocket of her blouse. She looks like a man and I don't like her. There's another lady there too, a social worker, my mum says.

'So, Lucy,' says the policewoman. 'I want you to take your time and tell us what your dad did to you last night.'

I know what's happening. I know what they want me to say and I know what will happen if I do. These are the stupid people. They are the ones who lock dads away and don't understand. Dad just got drunk and made a mistake. He doesn't deserve to go to prison. I hate what Dad did to me but I hate the thought of him going away even more. I will go home and tell him I don't want to do that ever again and I'm sure he won't when he knows I really don't want to. He's very clever like that; he understands me.

I am not going to tell them a thing.

'He didn't do anything,' I say calmly.

'Oh, Lucy!' wails my mum. She brings her hands to her mouth like she always does when she is really shocked.

I know if I say a word of what really happened, I will never see my dad again. So I keep pretending I don't know what they're talking about. I just shake my head and act like I don't understand. The policewoman continues trying to get me to say bad things about Dad but I keep telling her nothing has happened. Mum keeps on crying.

The policewoman eventually asks to speak to Mum outside and I sit alone with the social worker. She's a big, fat woman with long, greasy hair with grey bits in it. She has a long ladder in her black tights, and the heels on her shoes are all scuffed. She doesn't smell right either, and I move further away from her. She tries to talk to me herself but I pretend I haven't heard. There's no way I'm going to speak to *her!*

I hear Mum and the policewoman walk away up the corridor, and I continue to sit with the social worker for what seems like hours. Someone brings me a sandwich and some crisps and, even though I haven't had any breakfast and I'm starving hungry, I just ignore them. I'm not going to eat *their* food! I just sit with my arms folded, sulking. I look at the floor and try to block out the world.

After the longest time the door opens and my own dad walks in with another policeman. The policeman is someone I've seen before. He's a friend of my dad's called Malcolm. Dad and Malcolm are both laughing. I am so relieved, it's like a big weight has been taken off. I know now that if he's laughing it means Dad probably won't be going to prison.

I hear Dad say something about Mum suffering from depression; that she is 'on a lot of pills'.

'I know what you mean, Steve,' says the policeman. 'Sarah is the same. Bloody moody women.'

Dad tells the policeman that Mum had a lot of porn in the house and that I found it. He tells Malcolm that he had to get rid of it to keep it away from me. He then says Mum is a bit sexually 'fucked up'. He doesn't mention his own magazines.

'You poor sod,' says Malcolm to Dad. Then he says, 'Right, young lady. Time to go home with your dad. We're just going to talk to your mum a bit longer and then she can go home too.'

Dad takes me for a Wimpy burger on the way home from the police station. He says he knew he could trust me and that I need a reward for being such a good girl. He says he is so proud of me because I kept our secret. He tells me Mummy is a bit ill and that's why she has to take so many pills. He says she's a bit jealous because Dad and I are such good friends and that's why she wanted him to be locked away.

We sit and eat in silence for a bit. I'm desperate to ask him about last night, about what he did to me and why. Doesn't he remember? I know that sometimes people do stupid things when they're drunk, things they can't remember later on. Perhaps that's it: perhaps he simply can't remember.

But what if he gets drunk and tries to do it again? I can still feel what happened last night and it makes me shiver when I think of it. I have to talk to him about it so I can tell him I don't ever want it to happen again.

'Dad?' I say questioningly. 'Last night, when you–'

'Lucy, we can't talk about that here,' he cuts in, immediately. He promises me we'll talk about it later, at home. He says he will make it all better.

I feel a little happier as we drive home. I know everything is going to be okay because Dad says it will be. Dad always makes everything better.

Later that night the same friendly policeman brings Mummy home. He knocks on the front door, which is something no family member ever does. I don't think I have ever seen Mummy come in through the front door rather than the back kitchen door. This makes everything seem more serious somehow, like she's done something really bad. When Mum steps in, her face is all red and blotchy like she's been crying. Her hair is a mess and she looks old, like Granny.

'All home safe and sound. No harm done!' says Malcolm the policeman, brightly. Mum says nothing; she just pushes straight past Dad and shuffles upstairs.

'Thanks for this, Malc,' says Dad. 'I mean, it's all crazy. Just look at Lucy, does she look like a girl who's been badly treated?' They both look down at me. I smile up shyly: like an angel, a perfect picture of innocent happiness.

*I'm so sorry, Mum. I'm so sorry I didn't stick up for you when you were trying to save me. I'm so sorry I betrayed you with that smile. I would give anything to go back in time and take that stupid grin off my face. But I was so, so young. And he was so, so clever.*

*Dad had convinced me that he and I belonged to some exclusive secret club, for the most elite and intelligent people. He convinced me that we were the special ones, and that the rest of the world is stupid and ignorant.*

*It was almost as if I felt it was my duty to keep quiet.*

*Yes, that's kind of how I saw it. It was a great duty and an honour, and I wasn't about to neglect my responsibilities.*

# Chapter 6

The policeman leaves and Dad goes upstairs to talk to Mum. She's in the tiny spare room. He goes in and closes the door behind him. I hear their muffled voices coming through the door. There is no shouting. Dad is being kind to her, thank God. I can just make out a few words. Mum keeps repeating, 'Never again.' And Dad is saying, 'I promise. How many times do you want me to say it? I promise.'

Mum sleeps in the spare room that night. But at some point, after Dad has gone to bed, I hear her creep into my room. She gets into bed with me and falls asleep cuddling me, curled around my back like a coat. In the morning she is gone.

She must have gone back to sleep in the spare room on her own.

She doesn't go back to sleeping with Dad after that. Every night she goes to the spare room. Every night she creeps into bed with me, and early every morning she tiptoes back to the spare room. Sometimes I hear her go.

It's about a week after the visit to the police station that Dad finally speaks to me about the night he came to my bed. It's a night that Mum is working late and we have the house to ourselves. Dad tells me he only did what he did because he loves me so much. Sex is something that people do when they really love each other. It's how people show how much they care. He says he used to do it with Mum but now she won't let him because perhaps she doesn't love him any more.

I want to tell him that I never want to do it again and that I hate it. I want to be angry with him, but he always manages to make me feel sorry for him. I do feel sorry for Dad. I feel sorry for both of them. I wish they could be happy together again. Then I feel bad for being angry with him.

He says he's sorry if he hurt me but that the more I do it the less it will bother me. He says that when I have done it a lot of times I will start to like it. He says grown-up women love to do it. They love it so much they sometimes do it every single night.

I go quiet. Is he saying he's going to do it again? I don't think I could bear that.

'Dad, I don't want to do that again,' I say. And then I add, 'Perhaps when I'm older.'

Dad just tells me I *must!* He says I must learn sooner or later. He says if he doesn't teach me then some other man will have to do it instead. Dad asks if that's what I want. My heart starts to pound. The thought of another man doing that to me is horrible, it's one of the worst things I can think of.

'But, Dad, I really didn't like it at all.' I am close to crying now. 'Can you wait until I'm a bit older?'

'Yes, I suppose I can. If you really don't love me enough I won't make you.' He sounds really upset with me. I'm devastated that I have upset him so much.

'Dad,' I say, utterly shocked. 'I do love you more than anything in the whole world!'

'But, Lucy, if you really did love me, you would come to bed with me and do the things I want,' he says.

Then he tells me this is what all the really good and clever girls do with their dads. They don't tell everyone because they're good at keeping secrets, but lots of my friends do this with their dads too. He says he knows one of my friends goes to bed with her daddy all the time.

'Who?' I ask, wide-eyed.

'I can't say. It's a secret. I promised I wouldn't tell.'

'But I won't tell anyone, Dad. Tell me, tell me!' I'm desperate to know.

'Well, you have to *promise* never to tell anyone ever or Daddy will get in serious trouble.' I'm nodding, furiously.

'Well, you know Vanessa who's in your class? She does it with her daddy. She's been doing it for a long time. I even have a photo of her doing it that I could show you if you don't believe me.'

At first I'm astounded at what Dad is telling me. Vanessa Buckley is the prettiest, cleverest girl in the whole school. She lives in a really big, posh house and her dad drops her off at school in an enormous, shiny black car. She always has lovely clothes and shoes that click when she walks. We don't wear uniforms at my school, and Vanessa wears real Levi's jeans to school with a little orange label on the pocket. I am so jealous of those jeans. Everyone wants to be Vanessa's friend so they can go to parties at her house.

But it makes perfect sense to me that she would be having sex with her dad. After all, she's so clever and grown up. She's almost like a lady, and she has really neat handwriting. I would love to be like Vanessa Buckley. Perhaps if I have sex with Dad, I can be more like her and she will be my friend. Perhaps she'll even be my best friend.

'So, what do you say, Luce?' asks Dad. 'Are you ready to love your daddy properly, like Vanessa does?'

What can I say? How can I object? I don't even know *how* to say no to him. I am ten years old.

'Okay,' I say bravely, but I feel sick inside.

And my fate is sealed.

Dad now does it to me every time that Mum is working or out of the house. Often, Dad makes us look at photos first, 'just to get us in the mood'. I keep asking to see the photos of Vanessa, but Dad can't find them.

But I haven't started enjoying it at all.

I try to like it. I want to like it just like Dad says Vanessa does. But I still hate it. I really, really hate it. It feels weird and wrong and afterwards I sometimes feel sore for ages. Sometimes, I just want to be a normal, dumb little girl, not one of the clever special ones. Then I wouldn't have to do this with my dad. Afterwards, I always go really quiet and don't want to talk to anyone, not even Dad. At school sometimes I just start to cry for no reason and I can't think properly.

I don't feel happy any more like I used to. I just want things to go back to how they were before I looked in Mum's drawer. That was when all this started. This was all my fault; if I hadn't gone snooping around in their bedroom, I would never even have seen those stupid magazines.

Dad hardly ever goes in to work, and Mum is the only one bringing money in. Dad says Mum doesn't love him any more and never has sex with him. So he feels lonely a lot of the time. I don't want him to be sad and lonely and to feel that no one loves him. So I have to give him the love instead of Mum.

Sometimes I don't feel I have any love left.

*It fills me with rage that he made me think this. He made me think it was my duty to satisfy him sexually, because Mum wouldn't sleep with him. He made me feel it was my responsibility to fulfil his perverted needs.*

*I hate you for that, Dad. I hate you and damn you to hell.*

# Chapter 7

Mum doesn't know about any of this. I think she believed Dad when he promised never to take me to bed again. She takes a lot of pills now and she's asleep most of the time that she's not at work. She's really dozy all the time, and Dad makes most of the meals now. Sometimes she even forgets to go in to work and gets into trouble with her boss. Dad tells her she's going to get the sack if she carries on like this. Then she cries and puts her hands over her face.

Dad only does it to me when she's out of the house. He has told me not to talk to her about it ever. 'It would only upset her,' he has told me. I don't want to upset Mum. I don't want to upset anyone. I just want everyone to be happy again.

Then one day Mum comes home from work crying. She has been to a disciplinary meeting and has been suspended. She may lose her job because she's too unreliable. She's standing in the doorway of the kitchen when she tells Dad. Dad tells me to go to my room but I stop halfway up the stairs. I stay sitting on the stair, peering through at them. I don't think they know I'm watching.

I see Dad's hand come up and I think he's going to give her a hug; she looks like she needs a hug. But his hand comes high and he slaps it right across her face. She falls against the doorframe and hits her head on it. Then she drops to the floor.

'You stupid cow!' he screams at her. 'How could you be so stupid? Such an easy fucking job anyway, wiping arses and cleaning up vomit.' Mum is crying, but she's really quiet. The tears are flowing down her cheeks but she isn't making a noise.

I hate it more than anything when Dad hits Mum. I know he's really clever but I don't know why he has to hit her all the time. I know he only does it because she makes him so angry, but he could just shout at her or tell her off instead.

I try very hard never to make him angry because I am a little bit scared that he would hit me too if I made him angry enough.

Mum is home almost all the time now. She sometimes goes out to do a cleaning job that her friend got her. But mostly, she,s at home, sleeping in the spare room or lying on the sofa watching television. I often come in to find her sitting on the edge of the sofa, hunched forward over the coffee table, idly turning the pages of a magazine. She usually has a cup of tea half full next to her. Lots of our cups have chips on the rim and some don't even have handles. She doesn't pick out the nice cups to make tea; she just uses the battered ones. She usually lets the tea go cold without drinking it anyway, and she often then spills it.

The pills make her so dozy that sometimes she doesn't even answer when I talk to her. It's like she doesn't even know I'm there. She often drinks gin early in the day and she hardly eats anything. I haven't really spoken to Mum properly since the police station. Dad doesn't let her speak to me very often. Dad hardly ever leaves us alone together because he doesn't trust her to look after me. He hits her nearly every day now. She doesn't even cry most of the time.

I like Mum being home even though it makes Dad angry because he can't take me to bed when she's there. Sometimes, there are days and days when he doesn't have sex with me. I love those times. I start to feel normal again and almost forget about what he does to me.

One night Mum is asleep on the sofa downstairs when Dad says we can do it anyway, even though she's in the house.

'She's too drugged up to notice,' he says. He orders me to go upstairs and then follows me. As he's lying on top of me, I see the bedroom door open. Mum is standing in the doorway. She doesn't look dozy now. She looks wide awake. She has seen everything. Dad is naked and he is on top of me and she has seen everything.

I know there's going to be trouble now. Mum is in terrible trouble. Dad is in terrible trouble. I don't know what will happen. I just scrunch my face up, closing my eyes tight to block out the room.

'You *bastard!*' she screams at him. 'You sick, evil bastard! She's ten years old!'

Dad jumps off me and out of the bed. He is completely naked.

'Okay, calm down, Janice. It's not a big deal. Don't pretend you didn't know.'

'If I had known I'd have cut your bollocks off! What's wrong with you?' she says.

'Well, I wasn't getting any from *you!* What was I supposed to do?'

Mum just leans back against the wall and slides down it until she reaches the floor. She sits there and puts her hands over her face. Then Dad looks back at me. 'Lucy, go to your room. I need to talk to your mum.'

'*Promise* you won't hit her!' I am terrified of what he's going to do.

'It's okay, Luce. We're just going to talk, that's all,' he says to me.

I get up and pick up my clothes from the floor. I offer Mum a little smile as I leave but she doesn't even look at me. I leave the door open a crack intentionally and sit against the wall of my room, right by the door so I can hear what they're saying. I can just hear Dad say, 'You're the one that's sick!'

Mum wakes me up in the middle of the night. It's very dark and I only know it's her because I hear her whisper 'Shhhhhhhh!'

She gets me out of bed and very quickly gets me dressed. Then she tiptoes me very quietly downstairs holding my hand, very carefully taking one step at a time. She is very obviously trying not to wake Dad. At the foot of the stairs are a suitcase, our coats and her handbag.

'Where are we going?' I ask sleepily.

'We're going on a little holiday. But we just have to be very quiet so we don't wake Daddy.'

'Isn't Dad coming with us?'

'He's going to join us later,' she assures me. 'He just needs to get some sleep first.'

She goes to the front door. It's a mistake. We hardly ever open the front door and it's stiff. She has to give it a yank to make it open. When it finally opens it gives a loud shudder that seems to rattle the whole house.

In an instant, I hear Dad's footsteps pounding out of his room and in the corridor. Mum looks at me with a look of such horror. I have never seen her look so scared. She tries to herd me out the door with the big suitcase in her hand but he's coming down the stairs two at a time. Now Dad is here. He lunges at her, taking her face in his hand, pulling her back inside the house and slamming her up against the wall next to the doorframe. He shuts the door with his foot while she's still pinned against the wall by her throat. He puts his mouth very close to hers and speaks to her in a hissing voice, like a snake.

'You think I'd let you take my daughter away? Did you honestly think I would let that happen? Do think I wouldn't find you? I'd find you and I'd fucking kill you. I swear!' I'm so scared he is going to actually kill her. And I'm pulling at him, begging, trying to make him let go of my mum. But he doesn't pay any attention to me whatsoever.

He tells Mum he'll call the police and say I've been kidnapped. He tells her she'll go to prison. He tells her she's half mad and 'pumped up to the eyeballs on pills'. He says she'd never get custody. He says if they knew what sort of a mother she was they'd lock her up. He says she'd never see me again and that we'd be better off without her. Then he lets go of her and opens the front door again. 'Go on, you crazy cow, go! Do us all a favour.'

Mum doesn't move.

Dad makes me sleep in with him tonight. He says he doesn't want Mum anywhere near me because he doesn't trust her one inch.

A couple of days later, I come home from school to find a note on my bed. It's from Mum.

Darling Lucy,

You haven't done anything wrong. But I have gone away for a little bit. I can't help you at the moment because I need to do some things first. If Daddy does anything more that you don't like, you must tell someone. You can tell your teacher or your friend or Mrs Watts if you don't want to tell the police.

I promise one day soon I will come back for you. I promise this more than anything. Believe me, Lucy. I am coming back for you.

I love you so much,
Mummy

*I never showed Dad the note. I just hid it in a jewellery box on my bedside table where he wouldn't look. But I looked at it all the time. I read it every night before I went to bed and in the morning before I went to school. Sometimes I even carried it around in my pocket.*

*Mum said she was coming back for me. Mum wouldn't let me down.*

# Chapter 8

Now Mum has been gone away for weeks and weeks and I miss her so much. I wish I knew where she was so I could go and see her. I hope she's happy now that she's away from Dad and now that he isn't hitting her any more. I think about her all the time and I read her note over and over. Every day I look out the window to see if she's coming back for me.

Everything is different now she is gone. Dad still makes me watch videos all the time of men having sex with children. He still baths me and rubs the cream in but he makes me sleep in his bed a lot of the time now.

One night he invites his friend Brian around to watch videos, and he makes me sit with them while they smoke and drink. Brian brings some films of his own. Brian's films are horrible and a lot of the children in them look really scared and some are crying. Dad says those children just aren't taking their work seriously.

Then Dad has sex with me while Brian watches. Then Brian has sex with me too. I cry all the way through it. I am sick afterwards in the toilet but I don't tell them that. Dad says having sex with Brian is 'good training' for when I'm a superstar. You see, he's going to make me into a movie star. We're going to be rich. Brian and Dad and I are all going to be rich. And I am going to be a movie star.

But I don't feel excited about it. My tummy hasn't stopped churning since they told me. I can hardly eat anything, just thinking about it. I know this all means I will have to have sex with other men too, just like the girls in the films. That thought is so horrible I can hardly bear it.

I have my own plan too. Once I am very rich I am never going to have sex with anyone ever again.

I don't really speak to anyone at school any more. I'm not allowed to have friends to our house or see anyone after school. I feel very quiet all the time and not like talking, so everyone in my class just ignores me most of the time. I once asked Vanessa if she had a secret with her dad too, but she just looked at me funny and said, 'You're so weird.' I thought Vanessa was going to be my new best friend but she doesn't even talk to me any more.

Dad tells me he's organised a party for me, and he takes me shopping to buy me new clothes for it. At first I'm really happy and I'm so looking forward to it. But then he tells me it's not going to be that sort of party. No children are going to be coming, just grown-ups and me.

Tonight is going to be my acting debut. Dad says this means my first film. He says he's bringing some of Brian's friends around and that I am going to do a show for them and Brian is going to video it. Dad has bought me a new dress and new underwear and shoes. He has taught me how to do some dancing moves and I am to dance for his friends. I'm really nervous about dancing in front of strangers and I'm not really a very good dancer. But Dad says it doesn't matter. I don't have to do that sort of dancing. I ask Dad what else I have to do at the party but he just says, 'You'll be fine,' and smiles at me.

The friends are going to pay a lot of money and Dad is going to split it with Brian and me. I must do a very good job and work very hard, Dad says. This could be a real money-spinner, he tells me. This could be the answer to all our money problems.

Before the party, he talks to me and gives me my instructions for what I am to do. He tells me I have to be the best little actress I can be and that means not crying or complaining that I don't like it. He says this is what good actresses do. They pretend they are happy or sad or scared even though they don't really feel like that. This is what acting is. If I can do this, I will be a really great actress, like a real movie star, and earn a lot of money.

Dad dresses me in the new clothes. The dress is very short and the shoes have high heels that are quite hard to walk in. I hope I don't slip or fall over in them.

'If you don't know what to do, just smile,' Dad says.

'You don't need to say anything to anyone. Just do as you're told, put on a big smile, and that will be enough.'

Dad then produces another carrier bag from Boots. It has make-up inside. Dad puts lipstick and mascara on me and some blusher for my cheeks. He says I look like a princess.

'You're going to be amazing,' he smiles at me. 'My big, clever, special brave girl.'

I used to love it when he called me special and clever. But now I don't want to be special or different. I don't even want to be clever. I want to be like all the other girls at school. I don't even want to be grown up.

And I don't want to be a movie star.

Dad has got the house ready for the party. He's bought crisps and snacks and a big box full of cans of beer. He has moved the coffee table away from the middle of the room so that I can dance there. He brings down lots of the special magazines and videos from the bedroom and spreads them in piles around the lounge. He puts out dishes of crisps and puts all the cans of beer into a big tub filled with ice.

I hear the doorbell go. And I start to feel sick and scared. My tummy starts to hurt and I think I need the toilet. I go and sit in the toilet while all Dad's friends start to arrive. I lock the door and sit on the toilet with my pink towel wrapped around me. It's a rough towel, not fluffy and soft, but it's really big and wraps all the way around me. It feels safe and cool in the bathroom with the door locked. Perhaps they'll all get drunk and forget about me dancing for them. They might all be having so much fun that they don't notice I'm not there. I keep very quiet and I stay in there for a long time.

But Dad knocks on the door.

'Lucy, it's Daddy. It's time to come out now. The guests are ready for you.'

'I don't feel well, Dad,' I complain. 'I think I'm ill. We'll have to cancel the party.'

'Lucy, open the door and let me talk to you,' he orders. I don't have any choice. I can't hide in there forever. I eventually unlock the door and come out of the bathroom. I can hear men's voices murmuring downstairs. Some are laughing. I do want to do a good job for Dad, really I do. But I just feel so scared my tummy hurts and I feel sick. I try to stop myself but I start crying.

'Oh, Luce!' Dad looks worried now. Then he says 'Wait here,' and goes off to his bedroom. He comes straight back with something in his hand.

'I've had a great idea, Lucy.' He opens his hand to reveal a bottle of pills. I think it might be one that Mum left behind. Dad tells me that if I take one now then by the end of the dancing I'll feel really happy and relaxed and then I can enjoy the party. I hear someone coming up the stairs and Brian's head appears around the edge of the banister.

'She ready, Steve?' asks Brian. 'The guys are getting a bit restless.'

'She'll be there in a few minutes,' says Dad. Then he takes one pill out of the bottle and hands it to me. I really do like the idea of feeling really lovely rather than sick and scared. And I really want to make Dad happy. So I turn on the tap on the basin, take a drink of water and swallow the pill. Immediately, I feel a bit less nervous just knowing that soon I will feel better. I hope the medicine will work very quickly. Dad gives me a huge grin and hugs me tight. I still love him so much even though he isn't much like other dads. He takes my hand as we walk down the stairs together, walking ahead of me, holding my hand up like a lady, so that I won't fall over in my new shoes.

'Valium. Can't believe I didn't think of it sooner,' he says quietly to himself. I was right; those were Mum's pills.

Dad tells me to wait in the hall while he goes ahead of me into the lounge. I stand in the doorway while he introduces me.

'Gentlemen,' he says in a fake television presenter voice. 'Presenting, Little Lady Lucinda!' He opens the door to reveal me standing there, in my new dress, heels and make-up. Dad starts the record player, playing some music. I put my hand on my hip, just like he has shown me, and totter into the room. I don't look into anyone's eyes. I'm nearly choking with nervousness. So I just put on a big fake smile and begin the dance routine, just like Dad has shown me.

I do a particular little wiggle and some of the men clap. I'm amazed! I feel a little thrill of pride that they think my dancing is so good and I begin to feel a bit better. Maybe dancing for strangers really isn't so bad. Dad is right. The nerves are leaving me. I am even starting to enjoy myself. Maybe I will like being an actress after all.

Feeling braver, I look properly at the people in the room for the first time. There aren't nearly as many as I had expected, only five men plus Dad and Brian. There's a video playing with the sound turned down. Most of the men are smoking and drinking cans of beer. Brian is holding a video camera up to his eye, filming me as I dance. Everyone is watching me.

Dad puts on another record and, as instructed, I take my dress off while I'm dancing, clumsily pulling it down and kicking it off. I dance in my pants and shoes for another couple of songs.

By the time Dad tells me to take my pants off and dance naked, I think the pills are starting to work. I start to feel like everything isn't really happening, like I'm not really here – not really like a dream, but like it's happening to someone else and I'm just watching. Then everything starts to go blurry and cloudy and I feel dizzy. There's a kind of buzzing in my ears. I feel I can't stand up any longer and I want to sit down. I start to sway and stumble over on my high heels.

Then there are hands on me. Through blurred eyes, I can see naked white flesh everywhere. Stinking breath and the smell of bodies and dirty pants. More hands. Poking, probing fingers. Something is being pushed into my mouth. Wetness and that odd smell everywhere. Then nothing.

The next thing I remember is Dad carrying me up the stairs. Then he is lowering me into a warm bath. I can see the blue water from the Matey bubble bath. He washes me gently all over with a flannel. I still don't say a word; the drug is so strong I can't speak. He lifts me out of the bath, wraps me in a fluffy warm towel and dries me off. Warm pyjamas and into bed. Before he turns out the light, he kisses me on the cheek and says, 'My little movie star. You were brilliant tonight, Lucy. Just brilliant.'

I don't reply. I just fall into the deepest, blackest sleep of my life.

*I still remember the blackness, the drowsiness. I hate the feeling of drugs and alcohol to this day: the slipping out of consciousness, the dulling of senses.*

*As an adult I cannot bear to drink more than a few sips of alcohol or take medication that makes me drowsy. Even cough syrup causes me to panic. Whenever I feel even slightly drugged, I am taken back to that time.*

# Chapter 9

The next morning I wake up and all the men are gone. The house is tidy like nothing ever happened. I can hear the sounds of cooking. Dad is in the kitchen making pancakes with raisins for breakfast. He gives me a big smile as I come into the kitchen. I still feel like I'm not properly awake.

The kitchen table is laid out for breakfast and there's a big pink envelope with my name on it, propped up against the sugar bowl. I look at Dad.

'Go on, open it,' he says.

I sit down at the table and open the envelope. It has a picture of lots of balloons on the front with the words 'Well done' in big gold letters.

As I open the card, a note falls out. I recognise my dad's writing:

*Well done, my little superstar!*

*Love, Daddy*

I pick up the note from the floor. It's a twenty. Twenty whole pounds! I am shocked to see so much money.

'There's a lot more of that to come,' said Dad. 'Now eat up your breakfast and we can go out and spend it if you like.'

We spend all day out. Dad takes me to lunch and then to the pictures to watch *E.T.* The cinema is full of children and they're screaming and laughing with excitement at the film. But I don't really notice what's going on in the movie. I feel very quiet and sad, sort of empty. I think perhaps that medicine is still working because I don't feel like saying anything. My body feels very sore, like I've been doing a lot of running. Sometimes I feel I'm going to cry, though I don't really know why. When I look sad, Dad does something to make me laugh, make me feel a bit better. He doesn't talk about what happened last night after the pill started working. I don't ask him either.

Dad organises more parties with the same men. Each time he gives me a Valium tablet before I start to dance. Afterwards he bathes me and puts me to bed. In the morning there is always a twenty-pound note on the table in a card and he's making a special breakfast – pancakes, waffles or French toast. Mostly I don't want to eat breakfast in the morning. I don't know if that's just because I'm always so sad in the morning or because the pills stop me being hungry.

But the Valium makes things so much easier. I really don't think I would be able to work without it. I can't stand to think of what goes on; luckily, most of the time I can't even properly remember it because I'm so drowsy. Sometimes I sit at school and a picture will come into my head of a man's penis, or I'll remember the stink of men. And then I will start to cry in front of everyone at school. I can't imagine how much worse it would all be if I didn't take the Valium and I was wide-awake when the men are touching me. I think I would rather be dead.

I don't eat very much any more. I feel a sort of sickness in my tummy all the time. I must have lost weight because my school skirt slips down all the time.

My teacher says I need to eat something because I look like a beanpole.

Soon the parties are happening every Friday night, and he begins to invite more men, different men. The lounge is so full sometimes there isn't room for everyone to sit down.

I make up tummy aches and colds but he doesn't ever stop the parties. He just tells me it won't be forever and that soon we'll be rich. He says without this money he wouldn't be able to afford to keep me now that Mum isn't here to bring any money into the house. He tells me I will probably have to go into care if he doesn't sort out his money troubles. I don't argue with him when he says that. I don't think I could bear to be taken away and live in a children's home.

But then, perhaps I wouldn't have to do parties in care. Perhaps being in care wouldn't be so bad.

Dad buys me lots more outfits to wear to the parties and loads more shoes. I dress up like a princess with a tiara, or a movie star with a feather boa, or sometimes even like a baby wearing a nappy. I crawl in on my hands and knees with a teddy in my hand and sit in the middle of the floor, sucking my thumb like he has shown me to do.

Brian always takes the money. One night I am standing in the hall, waiting to make my entrance, and I see Brian sitting at the kitchen table. He has a big pile of money that he's counting and sorting into piles. It looks like hundreds of pounds, maybe thousands.

The very next morning I ask Dad about the big pile of money. I ask him why I only get twenty pounds when Brian was counting hundreds and hundreds of pounds.

Dad says I'm completely right and that I should be getting paid more for my hard work. He says the answer is to make more money so that we can all be paid more. He says it's time to 'step up the game'.

I don't know what 'stepping up the game' means.

I so regret mentioning the money, because since that day everything has got a lot worse. Dad has started driving me to strange houses with bigger lounges so more people can watch me dance and have a party with me afterwards. He has started arranging two parties every weekend, one on Friday and one on Saturday. On Sunday mornings there is now a fifty-pound note waiting for me at breakfast.

We have moved to a bigger, posher house. We have thick carpet everywhere, even in the bathroom. The lounge is bigger than the whole downstairs in our last house. The coffee table is made of glass and marble. The sofas are made of white leather and there's a statue of a full-size growling tiger sitting by the enormous TV. The kitchen is so big it has an island in the middle of it for cooking on. My bedroom has its own TV.

The parties are different now. I don't always have to dance and dress up. Dad doesn't always give me pills. He says some of the guests don't like it when I look drugged up. It's so much worse when I haven't taken a pill because it doesn't feel like a dream any more. I can feel everything that's going on and remember everything in the morning. I can smell the stink of the men, their bodies and their breath. I can taste it when they kiss me and put things in my mouth. But at least the parties are always at our house now that we have a bigger lounge. This means I can go straight to my bed afterwards.

There are some nights when I am not the only girl there. There are often two and sometimes three girls acting at the parties. One girl, called Jessie, is only six. The first night I meet Jessie she cries all night, from when she arrives right to the end. She comes to quite a few more parties after that but she soon stops crying. She doesn't make any noise or say anything at all now.

I don't know how many parties there have been. It feels like there is one every night, and all the days seem to blur together now. I'm dozy and sleepy a lot of the time, especially when I've taken the Valium. I often don't get up for school because I am so tired.

Dad always tells me how clever I am, but no one at school thinks I am. Almost all the girls can read better than I can, and I'm rubbish at maths. My most hated lesson is 'dictation' that we sometimes do with Mr Gravell. He reads aloud to us and we just have to write out exactly what he says. We have to get all the full stops and capital letters in the right places. One day it's so difficult that Mr Gravell says my handwriting is 'appalling' in front of the whole class. I am so ashamed that I feel really hot. One boy says, 'Lucy, you're blushing!' I just smiled and pretended I didn't care. But I was so embarrassed.

Some of the other girls and even the boys are allowed to use fountain pens and blotting paper. I'm so jealous when they get their pens and cartridges out of their pencil cases. I'm not allowed to use a fountain pen and have to just use a pencil so that I can rub things out when I make mistakes.

I'm good at art and swimming. I'm a fast runner and I always do the 100-metre race at sports day and I usually win. But I'm not good at anything else. And no one at school thinks I'm clever at all. Only Dad seems to think I am.

The teachers keep telling me I'm 'getting behind'. I get in trouble for missing so much school and Dad gets called in to see the headmistress. The secretary comes to my class to take me to the headmistress's office. All three of us are going to have a meeting about my attendance.

Dad sits next to me in Mrs Williams's office, holding my hand in his. He crosses his leg over the other with his legs apart, like men often do. I am really nervous. I feel like I'm in trouble and I don't know what Dad is going to say about why I have missed so much school. Mrs Williams speaks first.

'Lucy is really falling behind in her classwork, Mr Gilbert,' she says to Dad with a worried look on her face.

'Lucy has had some sort of virus, I think. We're going to get her tested for glandular fever, aren't we Luce?' I look blankly at him. It was the first I had even heard the words 'glandular fever'. Was I ill?

Dad is so polite when he speaks to people. He tells the headmistress how hard it has been for him since Mum walked out on us. He says Mum just abandoned me. Dad looks away from the headmistress and frowns, like he might start to cry. Mrs Williams looks at him with a sad look on her face. Poor Dad. He does look really sad. He must be really missing Mum still.

'What sort of a woman does that to a child?' says Mrs Williams to Dad.

But Dad tells her not to blame Mum because she had a lot of problems. She wasn't well in the head, he says, and she was drinking too much and taking a lot of drugs. He says he's trying to be Mum and Dad at the same time and that sometimes it's just really hard. Mrs Williams says she thinks he's doing a wonderful job.

After that meeting, Mrs Williams always gives me a little smile when she sees me around school. I never get told off. And when I cry sometimes, the teachers are really kind to me and just tell me to go and get a drink of water. Even though it seems like I'm only in school about half the time now, none of the teachers seem to mind when I miss a day any more. My form teacher, Miss Passingham, doesn't even ask for a note when I'm away from school any more

.

When I look back, I realise that not only did I struggle at school, but I also wasn't really a mature little girl at all. Dad told me I was so grown-up and clever. And because he was the only one saying it, I never wanted to let him down. I didn't want him to know the truth – that I struggled terribly at school, and even the other children thought I was babyish.

I wish I had told someone. I could have told Mrs Williams. I could have told Miss Passingham. Someone would have believed me.

But how could I tell anyone when I knew my Dad would go to prison, and my mum was nowhere to be seen?

# Chapter 10

There is a girl called Lydia who sometimes comes to the parties. She's a lot older than me, aged fourteen. Sometimes she acts for the film, has sex with the men and dances, but mostly she serves drinks and walks around with a tray with snacks on it. She carries the tray on the flat of her hand, like a proper waitress. She wears proper high heels and walks in them quickly and easily like a lady, without ever stumbling or tripping. She does all her own make-up and uses curling tongs on her hair. I think she is so glamorous. We always get ready together in my room and sometimes she stays over afterwards.

Lydia has become my best friend. She shows me how to put make-up on and talks about things that make me laugh. Dad actually likes Lydia and doesn't call her a 'common little bitch' like most of the girls at my school. Lydia is my best friend and my only friend. I really love it when she stays over in the spare room and goes home in the morning. That feels almost like normal life.

Dad makes us both breakfast in the morning before her own dad comes to pick her up. Sometimes she stays for the day and we watch cartoons or go into our huge garden and just walk around and chat about normal things. Lydia loves music and George Michael from Wham! She fancies lots of actors and people from the telly, especially Leroy from *Fame*. *Fame* is her favourite programme, and she wants to be a dancer when she is older.

Lydia tells me she's been doing these sorts of parties for years and years.

'But you must be very rich by now,' I say. She just snorts and says, 'Yeah, right!'

I'm watching a television programme one night when Dad is out. It's about adults who like to have sex with children, and mainly it talks about how bad and evil these people are. The lady on the programme says such men are perverts who prey on the innocent. Those TV people really are stupid and ignorant. Dad is right. Other people really don't understand. How can men who have sex with children be bad and evil if my dad is one of them? The TV programme talks of men who beat and kidnap children; it talks of paedophiles a lot – evil sick and perverted men who use children for their own sexual gratification. Not for one second does it cross my mind that my Dad is one of these people.

I think I have come to accept that I just don't get to have a normal childhood like others do. I am some different type of person – one who does not get to have fun, to laugh and play, because I have to work for my keep. I know our house is bigger and more grandly decorated than most of my friends'. I know my dad has two cars. But I know he is also very poor because he tells me all the time how little money he has. If I didn't do my work, he wouldn't be able to afford to keep me and I would have to go into care. That's how poor he really is.

It makes me sad to think that my dad is so worried about money. I hear stories on the television news about the 'poverty gap' and the way that some people can't afford to heat their homes or buy food. I know we're only a short way from being in that situation. So I work very hard for my dad to make sure we're never cold and hungry and so that I don't have to go into care. I love my dad so much and he loves me too. He's the best and the cleverest dad in the world. I just want to make him happy. I work hard so that he never has to shiver in a freezing house with no food.

But I do hate it so much that he has to have sex with me. I wish Mum were still here so that he would have sex with her instead. I hate doing the parties and doing my acting. Sometimes the men are so smelly and hairy and disgusting that I'm sick in my mouth and have to swallow it. I hardly ever eat my breakfast in the morning because I feel so sad. It's better when Lydia stays over because she helps me to take my mind off things.

I really wish Dad would let me have friends, even if they are stupid and common. I wish I could go to birthday parties like everyone else does, and have girls over for sleepovers. But Dad says he doesn't want me playing with their sort. He says the girls at my school aren't good enough for me. He says I belong in a posh, private girls' school, the type that royalty go to. He says that when we have enough money he'll take me out of that dump and put me in the best school in the country.

Sometimes I think it must be wonderful not to be special and clever like Dad and me. All the children at school who are just silly, stupid little girls don't have to work as actresses. But they look happy and they laugh and play after school and go to tea at each other's houses.

Sometimes I think I would rather be ordinary and stupid like them. Sometimes I even wish I had a different dad who still loved me but didn't want to do the things that my dad does. I see other dads picking their children up from school and sometimes I wish I was going home with them instead of walking home on a Friday night. I feel bad and guilty for thinking those things, but I can't help it sometimes.

*How is it possible to love someone who treats you so badly? All I can tell you is that it is perfectly possible. I felt such guilt even for wishing my life to be different. My dad told me he loved me and I believed every word he said. If I didn't like my life as a special, clever superstar then I was an ungrateful little brat. I thought that if I didn't like what those men were doing to me that it was somehow my fault. If I had been better at my job, if I had been more mature and grown-up and professional like all the other children in the videos, I would have enjoyed it more. That's how I saw it for a long, long time.*

*But things were about to change.*

# Chapter 11

I am walking home from school on Monday afternoon when someone taps me on the shoulder. I hear a voice say 'Lucy?' My heart jumps – I know that voice! I turn around to see Mum, standing right there in front of me with a big smile but looking like she might cry. I don't even think; I just rush into her arms and give her the biggest hug of my life. I am so happy to see her that I can't even speak.

Mum takes me to a little café near the school and buys me a Coke and a flapjack. She has a cup of tea and watches, beaming at me, while I eat. She looks different somehow – brighter, stronger. She looks like my old mum, the one I remember from early childhood when everything was still happy, before things started to go bad. We talk about normal things, school and television, about Dad's new house and about what she is doing. She tells me she's feeling much better these days. She has a new job, a good job as manager of a care home. She has her own flat and is earning good money. I'm so glad she's happy again. Perhaps Dad will let her come home now.

I stay about an hour with my Mum but it seems like just minutes. Just as we're about to part company I realise how desperately I miss her.

'Mum, please come and see me again,' I beg. Mum looks delighted.

'I would love that! I want that more than anything,' she says. 'But what about Daddy? He wouldn't like it. He doesn't know I'm better. If he found out I'd met you today he would be so angry.'

'I won't tell him,' I offered.

So we agree to meet again, same time, same place next week. I can hardly wait, and I look forward to it all week. She takes me to the same café again. Mum says it's a bit grubby but at least Dad will never think of looking there.

I meet Mum every single week now and Monday is the best day of the week. Even the weekend with two parties seems more bearable with Monday to look forward to. I start to call them 'Mumdays' instead of Mondays. I tell her this and it makes her laugh. I tell Dad I have a homework club on Monday afternoons. He doesn't like it but he doesn't stop me going. I am so glad.

I love meeting up with Mum. She's like a proper mum again. She's pretty and her hair is all tidy and beautiful. Her nails are long and polished and her clothes are smart. She seems as strong and clever as Dad now. Sometimes I think I would like to go and live with Mum instead. Sometimes after meeting her I don't even want to go home. Sometimes I think about running away with her and never going back to Dad. But I don't want to make him sad. Even though he does things that make me sick and unhappy, I still don't want him to be sad.

It's a few weeks before Mum asks me anything about Dad. I wonder why she didn't say anything sooner.

'So, Lucy. Tell me about Dad,' she says. 'How is he? Is he well?' I think she can tell by the look on my face that things are not okay with Dad. I don't say anything.

'Is he still, you know, does he still…?' I still say nothing. But she knows what the answer is.

'Does that make you very sad, Luce?' Finally I speak.

'Yes. It's horrible. But Dad's not the worst. It's the others I hate the most, all his friends.' Mum's face goes grey. She swallows, hard, and then swallows again. She squeezes her lips together very tight because they're trembling.

'What friends?' she says with a whispery, croaky voice. She isn't even looking at me.

Once upon a time I kept everything from her. But things are different now. She feels strong and so safe. Then, I'm telling her everything. I have never had anyone to talk to about this except Lydia. It feels so good to let it all out, to share the secret, to share the responsibility, to share the nightmare. I don't even care if the other people in the café can hear. I just tell her everything, every detail. I tell her about Brian, and the pills, and about Lydia and little Jessie. When I've finished speaking I worry that she's going to rage or cry or throw things about. But she doesn't even get angry; instead, she is very calm and just nods as I speak.

# DADDY'S WICKED PARTIES

'Lucy, I want to talk to you properly now. I want you to listen to me and try to believe that everything I say is the absolute truth.'

She says Dad has a way of making you believe things but that doesn't make them true. I think about that for a moment; it is certainly the case that Dad makes me believe things that no one else seems to agree with.

'I just always believe what Dad tells me and I do what he says because he's so clever, much cleverer than anyone,' I say.

'But he's really only clever when it comes to hurting people, Lucy,' she says. Mum explains that Dad is very *manipulative*, which means he can make people do and think anything he wants. It means he hurts people and makes them think it was their fault. It also means he doesn't even really think he is doing anything wrong. But that doesn't mean it isn't wrong.

'Lucy, what Daddy is doing *is* wrong. It is terribly, terribly wrong!'

Mum tells me that what Dad is doing is one of the worst things that any man can ever do to anyone.

Then she asks me how the parties make me feel. I tell her sometimes they still make me throw

115

up, and once I had to stay home from school because I was so sore I couldn't walk. I tell her sometimes it makes me cry just to think of them. She takes my hands and says no child should *ever* be made to feel sick and disgusted and sad like that. She says no child should have to work if they don't want to. She tells me the reason children aren't allowed to have sex is not because politicians are stupid. Children aren't allowed to have sex because they're bodies aren't ready.

Then she is saying sorry over and over and she sounds really sad again. She says she should have been stronger and stood up to him. She says that Dad made her feel like she was crazy and a terrible person and a bad mother. But she says everything is different now and she will never let me down again.

'Look at me, Lucy?' she says. 'Do I look mad to you?'

She doesn't seem stupid and mad any more. She sounds like she's telling the truth. I am so confused.

'I'll tell you what's crazy!' she raises her voice and looks angry for the first time. 'What's crazy is your dad and his friends, thinking it's okay to abuse children, when everyone else, millions and millions of people, the whole *rest of the world* knows they are wrong!'

Mum says that's the definition of crazy.

People are starting to look at us in the café. Mum tells them to mind their own business and then takes me out in the street to finish talking to me before I have to go home.

Mum tells me that if I came to live with her I would never ever have to have one of those parties ever again. She would not even let a man into the house if I didn't want them to be there. I would never have to have sex again until I'm an adult, and even then I won't have to if I don't want to.

I imagine life the way Mum describes it. It sounds like some kind of wonderland, like heaven, like magic. I could have friends around every single day for tea. I could go for sleepovers and have birthday parties where only little girls were allowed. I could spend a whole weekend just watching television or playing. No men. No sex parties. No sucking and poking and pushing and prodding.

And then, I don't want to go home. I don't want to go back to Dad, not ever. I don't care if I never see him again. I want to run away with her now and never go back home. When it's time for us to part, I cling to her and sob and beg her not to leave me.

'Please, Mum,' I sob into her, gripping her cardigan in my fists. 'Please don't make me go back!'

'Lucy, look at me!' she says. 'I *am* coming back for you. One day, very, very soon, I'm going to save you from all of this. But I have to be very careful. I have to make sure people believe me this time. The police think I'm a troublemaker and a liar because of that time when I called them on Dad and you said…' She stops speaking suddenly.

'I'm really sorry, Mum,' I say. I feel so desperately sorry that I lied to protect my dad. I got my mum into terrible trouble and I allowed him to carry on doing what he did instead. I have never regretted anything so much in my life.

'I know, darling. It wasn't your fault, really it wasn't,' says Mum. 'I know what he can be like. I've told lies for him too. Don't feel bad about that, not ever, you hear me? But from now on, you *must* tell the truth if the police ask you. You *must*. Can you do that?'

I can do that. There is no way I am going to tell lies for Dad again, not ever. I will not protect him any more, no matter what he says to me.

I want to go straight to the police now and tell them everything, but Mum says that might not work. It might even be dangerous. Mum says the police might just think she has put me up to it to get back at Dad. And if they don't believe us, she could go to prison. At the very least, if she got in trouble, we wouldn't be able to meet up alone any more, and then she wouldn't be able to save me. No, we need proper proof.

Mum says she has a plan. She's going to come home for a little while. But it won't be forever. It will just be for a little while until she can get Dad to trust her again. She tells me she might act a little bit weird and sometimes it will seem that she has forgotten about it. But I am not to worry. I am to trust her, no matter what she says or what she does.

She says when it's all over I will go to live with her, and that she will kill any man who tries to touch me again.

I look at my mother. She is a different mum from the one who left me months ago. She seems bigger than I remember and sort of powerful. I think perhaps I love her more than Dad. She's like a superhero; she's like Supermum.

*I remember walking home that evening feeling light, like I was floating. I felt excited and free, like everything was going to be okay and that the worst was somehow over, that a massive change was about to happen and that everything would be different very, very soon.*

# Chapter 12

That evening I think about everything Mum has said. I'm starting to think she's right about Dad and the way he makes people think funny things, and the way he makes them do anything he wants. I know we have this big plan to make me into a rich movie star. But the thing is, he never asked me if I *wanted* to be a movie star in the first place! That was his idea, not mine. And even if he did ask me, I'm still allowed to change my mind, aren't I?

I'm even starting to think that that TV programme was right when it said that what Dad is doing to me is sick and perverted. What he makes me do feels wrong, and it almost always makes me feel sick. That can't be right, can it? A lady on the

TV news says that no one, woman or man, should ever have to have sex if they don't want to. And I have to have sex all the time with people I hate, and who disgust me. And Dad *never* asks me if I want to do it. Dad never even seems to care when I'm sick or when I can't walk afterwards. I don't think that can be right. I don't think Dad is right about anything any more.

I have decided it's time to tell Dad I'm not going to do the parties any more. Somehow, talking to Mum has helped me find the strength to stand up to him. I know she'll be coming home soon so the parties will *have* to stop then anyway. And now that she has put the idea of a life without parties in my mind, I can't bear the thought of doing even one more.

I decide to tell Dad straight away that night, so he has a few days to get used to the idea. He will have to cancel the ones he has already planned. It's all over. I won't do another single one.

'Dad,' I say as we're having dinner that evening.

'Yes, sugar plum?' Dad replies.

Then I tell him everything. I tell him I've decided that I don't want to be a movie star any more. I want to be a vet. He knows I've always wanted to be a vet ever since I was little. I used to talk about it all the time before all this horrible business started. I tell him I'm not going to do any more parties. I hate doing them and I don't want to have sex with anyone, not ever again, not even when I'm a woman.

Dad frowns at me.

'I'm sorry, Lucy, but we can't stop just at the moment. I've got lots more booked and some people have already paid me a lot of money. If I cancel now we'll *both* be in a lot of trouble. You don't want to go into care, do you?'

For the first time ever I look at Dad and feel that I don't really like him any more. I feel the first little flush of anger. Just a tiny fire in my belly that makes me tighten up and grit my teeth. I want to tell him I won't be going into care because I'll be going to live with Mum and never have to do another party again. I want to say I'm going to tell the police the truth this time. But I know I can't say that because Mum made me promise.

Then I do something I have never done before; I answer him back.

'You can't make me!' I shout at him.

'Actually, I can,' he says quietly. 'Look, I promise we'll give you the pills every time for a bit.

123

I'll even give you an extra one so you can't even remember it in the morning, okay?' And then he adds, 'You'll be fine.'

Then I know. It's true: he really is a bad man. He doesn't care about me. He really doesn't care whether I am happy or sad. He pretends he does, but all he really cares about is the money. I run off to my room without even finishing my dinner and sulk for the rest of the night. Dad doesn't even come up to say goodnight.

*That night is when it changed. That's when I began to change. It's like I suddenly saw my dad from a different viewpoint, from a different angle, and in a whole new way. And I didn't like what I saw. He had changed in my eyes; I began to see him as the rest of the world does, not as a loving father but as a monster. And with that, my feelings toward him turned from pure love to the beginnings of hate. And when you have begun to hate someone, you can never go back.*

*For three decades I have despised my dad, and it all started on that very night.*

# Chapter 13

I come home one afternoon from school to find Dad sitting in the kitchen waiting for me. He has a strange look on his face. I know he has something to tell me.

'Lucy, I want to talk to you,' he says. 'I have some good news. I've been talking to Mummy and she's feeling much better. She's going to have a go at coming home and living with us, just to see if we can all get on again.'

'Oh, good!' I say with pretend surprise. 'I can't wait. When is she going to be here?'

I really hope he can't tell that I'm pretending to be excited. It's hard to lie to Dad. I always think he can tell. But he doesn't seem to notice this time.

Mum comes in that very night through the back door, just like everything is normal. She just has one bag with her, not all her stuff. It looks like she isn't planning to stay long, with just that one little bag.

I pretend to be amazed to see her, greeting her like I haven't seen her in ages. I play along and answer all her questions about school as if she didn't already know everything I was telling her. I cuddle up with her on the sofa like a baby and watch television. I'm so happy Mum's home that I don't even really need to pretend I'm excited. We watch *Are You Being Served*. I love this programme and Dad doesn't usually let us watch it because he says it's rubbish. He says Mr Humphries is a poof and makes him sick to watch. But tonight Dad just lets us watch it without saying a word. He seems in a really good mood now that Mum is back.

I don't want there to be any trouble yet. I just want to enjoy things for a little while. I feel differently toward my dad but it still feels nice having both my parents home to look after me – sort of normal. But I do wonder what Mum will say when she hears about all the parties Dad has planned. Maybe she has already talked to him about it. Maybe he has listened to her this time. Maybe he's cancelled them all.

Mum and Dad are really happy together for a while. They kiss each other and Dad sometimes pulls Mum off her feet into his lap. She squeals and laughs at him and calls him a big silly. They're sleeping in the same bedroom again. And they take me out like they used to; we go to the zoo and the cinema and out to lunch. A weekend goes by with no party, and then another. I start to feel happier and life is going back to normal, before all the sex parties started. Perhaps everything is going to be okay. Perhaps we won't even need to leave Dad. Perhaps he has learnt his lesson now. Mum can just stay home with us and keep me safe, and we can all be happy again.

But then, out of nowhere, they're talking about the parties. Dad is talking about how much money they bring in, and how many people like to come. But Mum doesn't lose her temper and there is no row. She doesn't even sound shocked or get angry. She just nods and carries on discussing things as if everything was completely ordinary and normal.

I'm really confused. She doesn't seem like the strong Supermum I've been meeting after school.

She's all kind of quiet and obedient to Dad, doing everything he says. She's more like the Mum who left, the one who was always drugged up, the one who wasn't strong and clever and safe. Mum says she just wants to be a proper family again and that she's going to let him make all the decisions from now on.

'I know you're right, Steve,' says Mum. 'It probably *is* good for her in the long run.'

I can hardly believe what I'm hearing. What does she mean: 'good for me'? Isn't she going to stop him? Isn't she going to stick up for me? Why isn't she protecting me? I don't understand. She did tell me she would say and do some strange things when she got back but I didn't expect *this.* I didn't think I would have to carry on doing the parties. After everything she said about how sick and perverted and wrong they were. Now she's talking about *helping* with them. What is she thinking of?

Perhaps Mum really is mad after all.

It's only a few Fridays after Mum moved back in. It's the Easter holiday and all the other children I know are excited at the thought of a big, long holiday, chocolate eggs and hot cross buns. But not me. Dad has planned a party for tonight and Mum is going along with it.

I don't know what to do.

I just can't do another party, I just *can't*. I could sort of cope while I was doing them all the time. I hated them but I just accepted them. But now everything has changed. Now I have imagined life without them and it's a life I want. I cannot bear to do even one more, not ever again.

I am desperate to talk to Mum alone, but Dad is always there. They go everywhere together now and are always talking and joking.

There is just one brief moment when Dad is upstairs in the loo that Mum and I are alone in the kitchen. I *have* to talk to her.

'Mum,' I whisper. 'When are you going to take me away? Why can't we just go now? I can't do the party. Please don't make me.' I start to cry.

'Lucy,' she says urgently. 'You *need* to trust me. *Please*, Lucy. I have it all planned. I know this is very, very hard but it's very important that we just act normally so that Daddy doesn't suspect ...' That's all she has time to say before we hear Dad's footsteps on the stairs.

And the moment he's back in the room, she's like a little lamb around him again, asking him if he wants a cup of tea and whether he'd like to watch the rugby. She even puts on a different voice around him, like a little girl. I'm so confused. I want to believe her but I'm a little bit afraid that she has gone really mad. Is she saying I still have to do the parties for a while? Is she not going to rescue me for weeks, or months, or years? Maybe she's never going to take me away at all. Maybe she's properly crazy now.

This party is on a Saturday and I can tell it's going to be a big one. They have got loads of drinks and food in, ready for all the guests. Mum has bought a new, sexy red dress for herself and some fishnet tights. She has really high red shoes that she can hardly walk in. Lydia is going to be there too.

On Saturday evening Lydia comes early. But I don't even smile at her. I feel like I can't speak. I want to hurry up and take the Valium just so that I can feel like everything is a dream. Mum gets me ready this time, and although she has the bottle of Valium in her hand, she doesn't give me a tablet.

'They're not good for you, Luce,' is all she says. Is she going to make me do the party wide-awake?

It is going to be unbearable.

I can't believe she's going to let it happen. She's been home for weeks and still she hasn't even talked about taking me away. She isn't stopping the parties at all. She's no better than Dad. I can't believe she has betrayed me like this.

She is shaking as she helps me dress. But I don't ask her why. I don't speak to her because I am so upset with her for letting me down. She's just the same as she always was. She just won't stand up to him. She does everything he says. She's weak and she's a rubbish Mum. She can't help me. No one can help me now.

She just keeps saying, 'Just trust me, Luce. It's going to be okay, Luce. You'll be fine, Luce.'

*But that's just exactly what Dad used to say.*

The doorbell starts to go and people are arriving. I can hear their murmuring voices and their laughing. I recognise some of them. I hear Brian's voice and the voice of one really disgusting, smelly man called Reg. I feel sick at the thought of him. He is the worst one of all.

It's really going to happen, all over again. I'm going to have those hands all over me. They will put their horrible things in my mouth. It will never stop. I will never escape this life.

I come downstairs alone and totter through the lounge door in my heels and a nappy. I have nothing on my top. I am an eleven-year-old girl, wearing a nappy and high heels. Even at eleven years old I know there is something not right about this. That TV programme was right. These men are sick, sick in the head. Dirty, filthy, sick perverts.

I look around but I can't see my mum. I haven't seen her since she dressed me.

There's a video playing. The video shows me being raped. The man raping me in the video is in this very room. I begin dancing, wiggling about. But I am not smiling. No one is going to make me smile this time. Lydia comes in with a tray of snacks. She is completely naked except for a pair of stiletto heels. I look at her and she looks back at me. There is a moment. A moment of sympathy, understanding, recognition. Lydia and I. Two little girls, childhoods cut short. Sold, raped, abused – all for the sick, dirty pleasure of a bunch of disgusting men who don't even have the decency to wash before they inflict themselves upon us. Mum has betrayed me. She has forgotten me. Lydia is my only friend now.

I hear an enormous bang and I jump almost out of my skin. Lydia startles too and drops her tray with a crash. Then the whole room seems to erupt, to explode. Every man is suddenly on his feet and there is panic and pandemonium. There's more banging. I just stand there, confused. I have no idea what is going on. Then I realise the banging noise is someone pounding on the front door. I hear someone shout, 'Open up. Police!'

Everyone is jumping around and shouting. Men are pulling up their trousers. Brian rushes to the video and starts pressing buttons, trying to stop the film playing. But the front door is open now. What seems like a hundred policemen are in the lounge. The film of me is still playing. Some men run into the kitchen to try and escape away through the back door, but there are more police at the back of the house too. One man starts fighting with the policemen and they all drag him to the floor and jump on him. One policeman kicks him.

Reg, the stinky man, is sitting on the edge of the sofa, crying and rocking. He is naked with his legs slightly apart. He looks idiotic and ridiculous just sitting there, crying, with his skinny penis dangling between his legs. He doesn't scare me any more; he just looks weak and stupid.

No one seems to notice me. I call to my mum but she is nowhere to be seen.

Then I catch sight of Lydia peeping out over the top of one of the sofas.

I sneak off to join her in her hiding place and we both watch the commotion from our place of safety. She squashes up close to me and doesn't speak.

It's not just policemen who have come in. There's also a policewoman there. I can see that Mum is with her. When the policewoman sees us, she comes straight over and crouches down to speak to us. I don't really hear what she's saying. Then Mum is there too. She's stroking my hair. She's not crying. She's just all breathless and trembling. 'Oh, my baby,' she says in a panting voice. 'It's all over now, my baby. It's all over forever now.' She smiles at Lydia and gives her a hug too.

Things eventually begin to quieten down. Lots of men are being put in handcuffs and taken out of the door. There is a lot of talking on walkie-talkies with scratchy beeps at the end of the conversations.

Eventually, Dad gets put in handcuffs too. The policeman is telling him he's being arrested for all sorts of things – all sorts of different crimes. When he's being taken away, Mum suddenly loses it like I have never seen her before. She starts to make a little noise like a tiny growl. As she stands up from the sofa, the growl becomes like a roar. She lunges at Dad. She punches him right in the stomach and he falls forward and coughs. No one stops her or pulls her back.

'I told you I'd get you!' she screams in Dad's face. 'You sick *fuck!* You delusional, evil, fucked-up *cunt!*' Spit is spraying out of her mouth as she shouts. I have never seen her so angry before.

'You want to know who tipped off the police? I did! It was *me!* Did you honestly think I'd let you do this again?' Then she says, 'You will never, *ever* come within a mile of me or my daughter again, not *ever*, you hear me, you *fuck*?'

'It's okay, Janice. We've got this now,' one of the policemen says to her. They take my Dad away.

*Mum had it all planned out after all.*

# Chapter 14

The police stay for ages, even after all of Dad's friends have been taken away. They are all being really nice to me and Lydia, treating us like we're very important. The policewoman's name is Pam and she's looking after us while the police are still doing things in the house. She takes us out to sit in the garden for a bit while all the policemen are doing their work and talking to Mum. She wraps us in thick, red blankets, even though we aren't cold, and we sit on the wooden bench by the back door. Pam brings us some hot chocolate with too much sugar in it and it's really delicious. Then she crouches down and tells us how brave we are and that we aren't to worry about a thing. She talks to us about normal things, about her own children and what it's like being a policewoman.

The police want to take Lydia away with them. But Mum says it's really late and she wants Lydia to stay with us for the night. Lydia gets really sulky and says she will just run away if anyone tries to put her in foster care. She says she wants to stay at Mum's with me. The police don't agree at first but Mum argues and argues with them and eventually they say it's fine.

When it's time to go, we go in the back door, through the house and out of the front door. I'm amazed: there are loads of people standing in the front garden and in the street, just watching our house. Some of them are police but most of them are just neighbours who have come to see what's going on. I recognise some of them talking to the police.

Lydia and I get in the back of a police car. We don't have any bags or clothes with us. Pam the policewoman drives us across town to Mum's flat. Lydia and I don't say a single word on the journey.

Mum's flat is so different from Dad's massive fancy house. It's small, and the kitchen and lounge are all one big room. But it's warm and really tidy and cosy. There's a French door in the lounge that opens onto a little garden. All the curtains and cushions look soft and flowery. There are photos of me in frames everywhere.

Mum has a bedroom already decorated for me, all in yellow – my favourite colour. There are two single beds in my room: 'one for your friends to stay,' says Mum. She gives us some t-shirts to sleep in and reads us a story before we go to bed. I think Lydia is going to say that the story is stupid and babyish, but she doesn't. She just listens to the story and then closes her eyes and goes to sleep.

The next day I wake up thinking there is going to be loads more going on. I imagine there will be police everywhere again and lots of questions. But it's not like that at all, and we just have a normal day together.

Mum tells me that after Easter the police will want to speak to us, and that we will both have to tell them everything. She tells me there is no need to be scared or nervous. But other than that, she doesn't mention anything that has happened all weekend. She just lets us watch cartoons and eat chocolate Easter eggs. On Sunday Mum does a big roast dinner for all of us. It is such a lovely Easter weekend with Lydia and my Mum. It's the loveliest weekend I have had for years.

Lydia stays with us for three nights because her Mum and Dad have both been arrested. One morning, a lady social worker comes round to speak to her about where she's going to live for now. I wish she could stay with us forever and be my sister. But after a few days she goes to live with her auntie, who really does love her.

When the time comes, I tell the police everything that has happened, right since the beginning. I tell the truth this time. But I don't go to the police station to talk to them. Mum takes me to a big house with offices in it. The policewoman who talks to me isn't even wearing a uniform, and she's really nice. No one asks me why I lied last time. My mum sits with me all the time that I'm talking. I don't feel scared at all. I feel really safe.

I thought I would be sad if ever my dad were to be taken away. I thought I would feel sorry if he was ever locked up for years and years. But once I know he isn't coming back, and it's really, truly all over, I am filled with the most amazing happy feeling; it's hard to describe just how wonderful it feels.

It's like I have been born all over again. Like Mum has just given birth to me and my whole life can start afresh. I feel like I'm flying. I feel light, bright, like an angel. But it's Mum who is the angel. She is my angel.

*Dad was clever. But Mum was cleverer. She had planned the whole thing. She had tipped off the police before the party and had helped to organise the raid where all the arrests took place. My mum was instrumental in sending my father and eight more men to prison.*

*She came back for me. She rescued me. She saved me, like she promised she would.*

*Lydia and I kept in touch for years. Eventually, she married and went to live in Australia. We lost contact for ages until she contacted me out of the blue on Facebook just last year! She is happy and has her own family now.*

*Mum has spent her entire life trying to make amends for her mistakes. I tell her there is no need, but she still feels the guilt, I think.*

*I have never seen my dad since the day he walked out of our front door in handcuffs over thirty years ago. That's okay with me.*

*I have known Kate Skylark for many years. We met as a result of our abuse histories. Kate has been a wonderful friend to me. She reminded me that everyone has their own demons, everyone has problems, everyone has worries and bad memories. But Kate told me that while we cannot change or put right the past, it is our choice whether to be happy in this very moment. The present is all we have and problems only live in the past or the future. They are almost never in our present. That idea has had a very positive effect on me.*

*There never really could be an entirely happy ending to my story. Nothing could put right the horror I endured over that short time in my life. But moment to moment, my life is a happy one now.*

*You know that song 'Everybody Hurts' by R.E.M? Lots of people think that's a sad, depressing song, but I love it. Whenever I get lost in the past, and imagining I'm the only one who suffers, I just remember to myself:*

*Everybody hurts, sometimes.*

*That helps.*

If you enjoyed this book, please check out

*Grandad's Funeral*

Another shocking childhood memoir
by Kate Skylark *with Emily Wilkins*

When eleven-year-old Emily is sent to stay with her grandparents in Wales for the summer holidays, she thinks it's all going to be one big adventure.

But Emily's grandad, the undisputed head of the family, the most respected man in town, has a dark and wicked side. And her life is about to take a terrifying turn.

When she returns home, Emily is too afraid to tell her parents the truth about her Grandad. And not wanting to upset her family, she carries with her the secret of what happened that summer for many years.

But finally, Emily gets the chance to take her revenge…

For every book sold,
a donation will be made to the NSPCC